BLINDING INSIGHTS
AND
BLIND ALLEYS

Glenn Pickering

TO SOW THE FALLOW SOIL

Winston-Derek Publishers, Inc.
Pennywell Drive—P.O. Box 90883
Nashville, TN 37209

PUBLISHED BY WINSTON-DEREK PUBLISHERS, INC.
Nashville, Tennessee 37205

Library of Congress Catalog Card No: 88-62110
ISBN: 1-55523-185-3

Printed in the United States of America

DEDICATION

This book is dedicated to Hugh Prather,
who showed me a format that I could use,
and to Gwen, who showed me herself.

I am often confused, scared, and unable to find my way. Yet a close friend recently described me as being competent, organized, and self-assured. This description left me with mixed feelings. On the one hand, I was pleased to know that this person thought so highly of me. On the other hand, however, I was sad, because I obviously had not allowed my friend to see all of me.

In the past, I spent far too much of my time "proving" that I was totally competent. Only now do I realize that my efforts resulted in the worst possible outcome—people believed me.

To reveal oneself is to invite revelation by others; thus it is the gateway to giving and to intimacy. To conceal oneself, on the other hand, is to encourage others to conceal themselves as well; it is therefore the means by which we cut ourselves off from life, and condemn ourselves to isolation.

I am striving to choose revelation, that I might rejoice in its life-giving power.

Self-revelation can be scary. However, to conceal myself is to deprive myself of life's greatest experience—being loved for who I really am.

There are indeed people against whom I must protect myself. However, these people are in the minority, and I make a grave, life-limiting mistake when I assume otherwise.

I want to be the most I can be—not by absorbing others, but by giving to others. I want to give to people the type of love that enhances, that helps them to become all that they can be.

Erich Fromm noted that giving often was perceived as a sacrifice, as "giving up" what we possess.[1] But the giving of love is a giving of the self, and thus is a giving that enhances, rather than impoverishes, me. To give of myself is to create the possibility of being united with another, and that makes me richer, not poorer.

To engage in sexual encounters with an endless list of partners is not love, for it is not a giving of the self. It is, rather, a taking and a superficial escape from self-revelation. Such activities, rather than binding us together, actually separate us from ourselves and from others.

I do not mean to proclaim self-righteously that "no one should engage in sex unless they are 'in love'." My point, rather, is that when sex is not a gift it can not provide the sense of oneness that is life's ultimate miracle.

Several years ago, I went through a very difficult time, a time when I no longer could pretend that I "had it all together." I was forced to lean on the people around me, and I found that, when I allowed them to, my friends were unbelievably good at taking care of me. In fact, even a person that previously had seemed to me to be totally self-centered showed remarkable compassion.

After all those years of being the "strong giver" and of fearing vulnerability, I found that being a vulnerable receiver was a moving experience. Much to my surprise, it felt really good to let my friends take care of me for a while.

Now that have put the pieces of my life back together, I want to continue to be a gracious receiver, as well as a caring giver.

To give of myself does not mean that I cannot receive, as well. In fact, to be totally giving means that I must allow others to see my needs, as well as my skills; my weaknesses, as well as my strengths; my fears, as well as my caring.

I once had a neighbor who was an ardent supporter of homosexuals, blacks, and many other oppressed groups. He made speeches, attended rallies, organized letter-writing campaigns, and described himself as "a man who cared deeply about others."

Unfortunately, he also played his stereo so loud that it kept me awake all night.

Lately, in a number of situations, I have been very honest, direct, and emotionally real. In other words, I have been the kind of person that I really have wanted to be.

After many of these occasions, I felt not only pleased, but also powerful. It was as if all along I had been playing basketball but had agreed to play at only half speed. Now, with my decision to be more authentic, it was as if I suddenly had started to play at full speed; I felt lighter, faster and very strong. What a treat!

If I wish to have a meaningful relationship with someone, I must be willing to express my feelings honestly. Such honesty, however, does not guarantee a successful interaction. Some people are simply uncomfortable with emotional closeness, and will react accordingly. Others, who generally would welcome such closeness, will, on occasion, react badly to my attempts to be direct and honest.

My tendency, after such an encounter, is to draw back, to cease in my attempt to be more authentic. It would be more helpful, however, for me to see these occasional difficulties as the minor setbacks that they are, and to forge ahead. Life, after all, comes with only one guarantee: when we quit growing, we die.

Often, when I first meet someone, I am so busy trying to think of "what to say next" that I run out of things to say.

Conversation is a lot like sex. It's awkward at first, but when it's good, it flows smoothly and spontaneously from one moment to the next.

When I am around those who wear the thin veneer of juvenile sophistication, I become painfully aware of my own separateness. I know that if I deviate from their norms, they will deal with me swiftly and harshly. Thus, the choice is either to join the herd or to suffer the consequences.

To be an adolescent is to be trapped in such a world of rigid expectations. To be a mature adult, however, is to accept others as they are, and to rejoice in their diversity. Only then do self-disclosure, love, and unity become real possibilities.

Given the fact that mature love rejoices in diversity, can God be the divine teen-ager, the all-powerful enforcer of our social norms? Hardly. God, rather, is the one who accepts us as we are, who always loves us, and who calls us to care for one another with the same kind of steadfast love.

Gwen's love for me has helped me to see that God's love for each of us is most clearly expressed in our relationships with others. When two people truly connect with each other, the love that flows between them is literally a gift of God—an expression and experience of God's essence.

We Christian theologians are fond of saying that what made Jesus unique was the fact that he was part mortal and part God. Yet, isn't this true of all of us? To be human is to be part animal and part spirit, which is why it is possible for us to experience the love of God, in our relationships with others.

The fact that each of us is part spirit implies that each of us has a tremendous responsibility. It means that each of us is called to be, in some small way, God-on-earth.

Thus, as children of God, we do have a duty. But the duty is not an unthinking obedience to a simplistic list of *do*'s and *don'ts*. Rather, the duty is to give of ourselves and to love without reservation. In this way, all people might come to know the love of God and be healed.

Hell is not a place "down there" where evil people go. Hell is a life without love.

People often talk about "God's plan" as if it meant that their most minute behaviors were preordained and thus *had* to happen. To me, this attitude seems like an attempt to take the easy way out, to avoid doing what needs to be done. It seems to me that God's plan is indeed a plan. It is a dream, a vision of what could be, rather than an already accomplished fact. As such, it requires our active participation. Without our help, the plan will remain just that—an empty awareness of what could have been.

Many people prey upon our doubts by offering us "certainty." Some religious groups, for example, promise to show people "the one sure way to heaven." The appeal of such a promise is easy to understand. In a world filled with ambiguity, it can be very refreshing to believe that something, anything, is clear, sure, and certain.

Unfortunately, the price of such "certainty" is high. In order to be a "believer," one must accept the opinions of another and must pass them off as facts. One also must quit thinking for oneself and thus must quit asking difficult questions.

The irony in all of this is that it is precisely our questions that keep us in touch with the mysteries of the universe. Consequently, to settle for certainty is to distance oneself from God.

Even unanswered questions are better than the ignorance that comes with certainty.

Beware of those who know all of the answers.

Life is filled with ambiguity. To pretend otherwise is to deny our own reality and to condemn all those who are "different".

When I think back to my childhood, some of my clearest memories are of the times when I was punished unfairly. For example, I remember my kindergarten teacher scolding me for something that I did not do. I also remember being harshly criticized by my peers for making an honest mistake, a mistake born of confusion, not of malice.

To this day, I carry with me the feelings of anger and shame that those situations created in me. This resentment, of course, represents a tremendous waste of energy and effort, a trainload of excess baggage.

What can I do now to lighten my load? I can think of each of those persons not as "awful" or "unjust" but as human beings who made a mistake. And I can forgive their mistakes, just as I want others to forgive mine.

My capacity to forgive the sins of another begins with the realization that I have either committed or been capable of committing the very same sins.

Thus, in order for me to forgive others, I first must forgive myself.

Forgiving myself does not mean finding a rationalization for my behavior. Rather, it involves acknowledging my flaws and accepting myself, flaws and all.

When I freely admit my own mistakes, or when I listen nondefensively to a person who is criticizing me, I do not feel bad or less worthy. Rather, I feel free—free of the shackles of trying to appear perfect.

We often are rewarded for doing those things that are important to the rewarder, rather than to us. For example, my employers and teachers reward my "workaholic" behavior by giving me more money, lavish praise, or better grades. For accomplishing tasks that *they* deem important, I receive many different rewards.

Unfortunately, when I am a workaholic for a while, my personal life deteriorates. Gwen feels distant from me, friends drift away, and hobbies get neglected. Thus, when I chase too hard after the external rewards offered by others, I find myself missing out on all of the internal rewards, the things that are most important to me.

Everyone likes to have some of the externals, such as money and prestige. And things like a home and transportation are, in fact, important. But when my life is filled with nothing but externals, my life is empty indeed.

Some days I am like a whirlwind. I get so much done that it amazes me. At the end of such a day, I invariably feel like I can not wait until tomorrow, when I can be a whirlwind all over again. And just as invariably, when I get up the next day, all I want to do is to take it easy.

Apparently, even when I consciously try to override it, there is a built-in part of me that knows there is more to life than simply putting my nose to the grindstone.

A professor of mine once said, "the concept of a career is a retrospective concept." It seems to me that much of life could be described in the same way. Despite my best efforts to control the future, I can not predict where my life's journey will take me, and it is only in retrospect that the journey seems logical and orderly.

So often, all of my "big plans" come to nothing. So often, great things happen that I did not plan. Since I know that these things are true, why do I keep on making "big plans"?

Right now I am depressed because one of my biggest plans of all did not work out. In truth, though, I am no worse off now than I was before. So why should I feel depressed? I suspect that it is because I have once again been shown just how little control I have over certain events, a reality against which I try desperately to defend myself.

One way for me to avoid the frustration of plans that do not work out is to live more fully in the present. Sometimes the best way to maintain my long-term ability to cope is to not cope—to enjoy the sunshine just because it's there, to eat, just because it sounds appetizing, to make love just because I find my partner irresistible.

I often look back on my life and think "I am so much more mature now than I used to be." I'm like Beverly Cleary's character Ramona, who, when she entered the first grade, looked down her nose at the "kindergarten babies."[2] I always think to myself, "Well, now I really am all grown up." Then I take stock of myself at a later date and find that I once again have grown even further, leaving the "mature" me far behind.

I always think that I finally have arrived, only to find later that I never stopped moving.

Even in the midst of the apparent clutter there is always movement; life is always moving forward.

This movement is not discrete, but continuous.

Changes that appear to be abrupt often are not.

Although life is characterized by change, its many changes ought not blind us to the fact that there also is an underlying stability or pattern of which we often are unaware. Sometimes transitions are more illusory than real.

The more I change, the more I stay the same.

I used to wax philosophical about the transitory nature of life. I would get upon my soapbox and complain that friendships seemed so temporary. As an example, I would recount how I talked to certain classmates every day during school, but after graduation, nothing.

Well, yesterday I had dinner with an old school friend. Although we both admitted being a bit nervous, the conversation flowed smoothly, and our time together passed quickly. It was almost as if we never had been apart.

So much for my "life is transitory" theory. As it turned out, the transience of our relationship was due only to my own lack of effort.

Tomorrow I'm going to call or write to every friend I've ever had.

If I spent more time looking up old friends and less time planning my future, I probably would be better off.

I feel as though I have become wiser recently. It's not that I feel smarter or more learned. It's more a sense of knowing who I am and who I am not, and being content with that.

Gwen calls me "a hick from the city," and that is pretty accurate; although I grew up in a metropolitan area, I am a terribly unsophisticated person. During my high school and college days, I saw my "hickness" as a major liability. So I tried (unsuccessfully, of course) to be worldly and "cool," in an attempt to make people like me. Of course, few people did. Now that I act more like the hick that I really am, people generally do like me. There's a moral there, somewhere.

I am changing. However, much of what is changing is not my essential self, but my willingness to be true to that self.

A while ago, I wrote, "the older I get, the more like myself I become." I loved that thought and felt that I had characterized the growth process in a powerful and unique way. Later, I discovered that Hugh Prather had written virtually the same thing years earlier.[3] Perhaps I should have said, "the older I get, the more I can see that my experiences parallel those of everyone else."

All of us are unique, and all of us are exactly the same.

The more like myself I become, the more spontaneous I become. I used to feel like an observer, watching life from the outside. Instead of simply telling someone that they looked nice, for example, I would try to find the "right" way to tell them, or I would not tell them at all. Now I am more free to compliment people, to touch people, and to love people.

Such spontaneity entails a certain amount of risk, of course, but nowhere near as much as I once believed. Once again, I have discovered that the fears that previously had incapacitated me were quite unrealistic.

Almost any time I try something new, I find that all of my prior rationalizations for not engaging in that activity were exactly that.

For me to grow, I need to take risks, I need to be willing to change. It is safer, certainly, to stay the same. However, like all forms of safety, this is not life, but rather a slow death.

On any given day, we each are assigned to play a variety of roles—teacher, male, adult—and are expected to act in ways that are consistent with those roles. We assign such roles to one another because the roles make our world more predictable and, therefore, less frightening.

However, those roles also can suffocate us; they can keep men from expressing their emotions, adults from being childlike, and members of the clergy from being human. Clearly, we pay a high price for predictability.

Many people seem to think that it is their personal duty to make sure that their minister, priest, or rabbi never strays from his/her role. It's no wonder that so many of my clergy acquaintances are better at being ministers than they are at being people. And it's no wonder that they remain acquaintances, rather than becoming friends; it's hard to be perfect and to be a friend at the same time.

All too often, people equate "ambitious" with "ruthless," as if having lofty goals necessarily implies that one has to step on others in order to reach those goals. However, to me it seems entirely possible to have a clear sense of direction and to be gentle at the same time.

Like all people, I have been blessed with certain gifts. The more I come to know myself, the more clearly I can see the areas in which I am gifted and the more motivated I am to use those gifts to the best of my ability. My ambition, therefore, springs not from a desire to be better than others but from my acceptance of myself and from the intensity of purpose which that acceptance engenders. Perhaps this is what Carl Rogers meant when he spoke of our drive toward self-fulfillment.

At any rate, it is clear that my most powerful ambitions now are based not upon the desire to conquer those who are outside of me but, rather, upon the desire to express that which is inside of myself.

Just as ambition does not rule out gentleness, so, too, can beauty coexist with order. It is only when we emphasize one, at the expense of the other, that the complementary nature of their relationship is obscured.

In order for me to have a clear sense of direction, I must have time for inactivity and reflection. Direction comes not from fevered activity but from a clear sense of self. In order to gain self-knowledge, I must spend some time with myself.

A life without purpose is too painful to contemplate. Perhaps that is why people who have no sense of purpose so often choose to be constantly busy. Intense activity creates the illusion of purpose and also prevents one from having to acknowledge the illusion.

It is one of life's painful ironies that those people who use their constant business to avoid confronting their lack of purpose are thereby prevented from gaining precisely that self-knowledge which would lend meaning to their frantic activity.

Filling an empty spot does not eliminate the spot.

When I am deprived of my time alone I become anxious, depressed and overly-concerned with the opinions of others. This makes perfect sense: when I get out of touch with myself, I focus too much upon what other people think. Seeing the judgments of other people as more important than they really are makes me vulnerable to the whims of others, which leaves me feeling anxious, out of control, and depressed.

Life can be viewed as a series of parallel lines. I live my life here, while at the same time you live your life somewhere else and billions of others lead their own lives, totally unaware of you and me. It is only because we are egocentric that we think of life as a single (straight?) line. In reality, there are many parallel lines and lives, all occurring simultaneously.

I often consider life and people to be divisible into categories or threads. While this is a legitimate perspective, it is also the case that these apparently separate threads combine to form a single bolt of cloth.

It is a bit like the phenomenon of light. Physicists have found that although life consists of a series of energy "packets", it is also a continuous wave. As yet, no one completely understands this apparent paradox, but we do know that both aspects of the paradox are true.

And so it is with life; you can analyze the separate drops, yet it is all one river.

A professor of mine once said, "people fall into two major categories: those who divide everybody into categories, and those who do not." 𝄽

Child psychologists tell us that when an infant no longer can see an object, he/she assumes that the object no longer exists. These same psychologists assure us that once a child reaches the age of two, he/she no longer makes this error. Personally, I am not so sure that we ever quit making this egocentric mistake. Like an infant, I tend unconsciously to assume that the people I do not often see do not exist during the intervals between our visits. It is only when I go to visit my geographically distant relatives, for example, that I become aware that their lives have continued during my absence. Similarly, I find it hard to reconcile myself to the fact that all of my childhood playmates are grown-ups, are married to people that I do not know, and have children of their own.

The old saying, "out of sight, out of mind," indicates what people have always known—we adults are not much different than those infants.

In life, balance is very important. However, it is not all-important, and it can be attained in a variety of ways.

Life is filled with innumerable small pleasures, and our occasional major setbacks ought not blind us to that reality.

The sight of a sleeping child rarely fails to move us, in part because the child's vulnerability and gentleness show through in a way that is hard to ignore. We say wistfully, "he/she looks so innocent," and we long for a return to the days when we, too, were that innocent.

In truth, however, we need not mourn our lost innocence, for each of us possesses exactly the same gentleness as does that sleeping child. Obviously, we can not return to the days of our childhood. But, we can strive to get back in touch with our own gentleness, and we can strive to let that gentleness govern our relationships with others.

Love is not static. If all goes well, it ripens; in place of newness come favorite traditions, in place of thrilling uncertainty comes security, and in place of mystery comes a deep knowing.

Few people who have known mature love would consciously choose to trade it for the thrill of falling in love. Yet, even for such people as these, the lure of a new romance can be very powerful. Many people initiate extramarital affairs in a destructive attempt to have *both* the mature love of a long-standing relationship and the excitement of a new one.

Many people lie to themselves, saying, "This affair will not damage my marriage." This attitude is indeed a lie, because an affair brings an element of secrecy into the marriage and steals some of the time and some of the energy that a successful marriage requires. However it is a popular lie, because it leaves people thinking that they really do not have to decide.

Life is full of choices.

We can strive to make the best choices possible, but we can not avoid having to make choices.

Gwen's spontaneity and infinite curiosity have taught me that there always are new areas to explore, new aspects of her, me, and us to discover. By her example she has taught me that there is indeed one way in which a person can have both a mature love relationship and the excitement of a new relationship—by having both with the same person.

When John says "our relationship is boring; I know everything there is to know about Sonja," his boredom is not a sign that there is nothing new left for John to find. Rather, it is an indication that he has stopped looking.

All it takes for a relationship to fall apart is nothing.

It often has been said that a person needs to be a strong individual before they can be a part of a strong couple. Paradoxically, it also is the case that being a strong individual is something that can best be learned in a meaningful relationship.

Existentialists are fond of noting that each of us is ultimately alone. I agree that this is the case. However, it also is the case that those of us who can acknowledge and accept their separateness are the ones who are best able to be connected. This truth is another of life's little ironies; by rushing blindly from one relationship to another, in an attempt to avoid acknowledging our separateness, we eliminate the possibility of overcoming our separateness.

Our separateness and our need for love are not contradictory. Each enhances the other, and each requires the other for its fullest expression.

I used to pride myself on being a rational, pragmatic person. So, I was always a bit skeptical when people talked about "the rhythm of life" or about "doing everything in its own time." However, my relationship with Gwen has unfolded in such a natural way that I now am more sympathetic to such notions. Instead of hurrying our relationship, or forcing it to go in some preconceived direction, we were able to let it develop naturally, and I will be damned if that process did not prove to me that life does indeed have its own natural rhythm.

Apparently, my life really is most satisfying if I do not force it to progress more quickly than is natural. As Ecclesiastes says, "For everything there is a season" (3:1).

Recently, two of my friends were arguing about whether or not they should get married. She wanted to get married right away, while he had a million reasons for putting it off. She argued rationally against his *stated* objections and thereby missed the point entirely.

I now believe that anyone who puts off getting married is right to do so, not because their reasons are unassailable, but because a person who does not feel ready to be married is not ready to be married.

I know a number of Christians who act as if this life is of no importance, as if the afterlife is the only meaningful portion of our existence. They appear to have lost sight of the fact that life is a miracle; it is a gift from God that we are called to enjoy and to use wisely. In their emphasis on the future, to the exclusion of the present, they are like the bride who had her hair in curlers during the wedding, so that it would look nice for the reception.

Life is meant to be lived.

I suspect one reason people tend to overemphasize getting to heaven is that it helps them to maintain a feeling of being in control. Perhaps they think, "If I behave in certain ways, I know that I will be admitted into heaven," which puts them in control of their own destinies and in control of God's love.

In truth, however, love is a gift, and gifts are freely given, not earned.

Some people have said that a friend is someone who accepts you as you are. But it also has been said that a friend is a person in whose presence you must change. Although these sentiments appear to contradict each other, it seems to me that both are accurate.

If you accept me as I am, then I need not bother to defend myself or to protect myself against you. I therefore can admit to you and to myself that I am imperfect, which frees me to respond to my strong, innate desire to be better, to be all that I can be. Thus, a friend is a person whose acceptance triggers a strong desire in me to change. Love frees us enough that we can demand change of ourselves.

I can not teach you anything that you do not already know. However, I can point out or clarify some of what you do already know.

There are no shortcuts. I can not give you my experiences, nor can I spare you from your unpleasant ones. I can, however, help you to make sense of the experiences that you have had, just as you can help me to make sense of mine.

My students often act as though I have or should have all of the answers. In reality, however, I have many more questions than answers. If I could teach my students only one thing, I would teach them that learning to ask their own questions is far more important than learning my answers.

My goal as a teacher is to *start* a person thinking, not to do their thinking for them.

At heart, I always have been and always will be a teacher; I simply love to be a part of the learning process. Lately, however, I have been feeling a bit dissatisfied with teaching, in part because I have been trying to force my students to learn. Instead of forcing students to learn, what I want to do is to kindle within them the desire to learn. If I can do that, they will not need me to coerce them. In fact, they will not need me at all.

A person who truly wants to learn can teach himself/ herself almost anything.

No matter how sorry I may feel for myself in a particular situation, the fact remains that life is an opportunity, not a chore.

Yesterday, David said to me, "I don't like John." When I asked him why not, he cited several of John's annoying habits and concluded by saying, "and besides that, John is a snob." While I had to agree that such characteristics could indeed be obnoxious, I could not help but point out that many of David's friends exhibited similar flaws and that in their cases he seemed willing to overlook those same imperfections.

We all are a mixture of good and bad; our friends notice the good parts and overlook the bad, while our enemies do the opposite. Thus, it seems to me that the differences between our friends and our enemies tend to be more perceived than real.

This difference in perceptions leaves me with two thoughts. First, it makes me think that if we chose to concentrate on each person's strengths, we could indeed love everybody. Second, it points out that our "reasons" for liking or disliking a person tend to be after-the-fact rationalizations. That is, although we act as if we have factual reasons for our likes and dislikes, our reactions often come first, followed by our reasons.

Ugliness, like beauty, is in the eye of the beholder.

The more completely I know someone, the more likely I am to care about that person.

It could be said of all people, "and they were made flesh and dwelt among us."[4] Unfortunately, as Jim Nelson—the author of *Embodiment*—has suggested, many people in our culture have become distanced from their bodies. They equate "physical" with "sexual," define sexuality in purely genital terms, feel that they can express themselves sexually only in that way, and then pass laws that make even certain forms of genital sex illegal. The results are a painful lack of physical spontaneity and a vague feeling of guilt towards all things sexual.

Oddly enough, in our society, the male athletes, who often are quite macho and uncomfortable with sexuality between males, are the ones who get to hug each other in public.

Perhaps these athletes are able to be spontaneous in expressing their physical and affectionate responses during their games because they are wearing their pads and therefore do not actually touch each other's bodies. As evidence in support of this theory, I would point out the fact that very little hugging and butt-slapping occurs in the locker room and that athletes such as basketball players, who wear very little armor, tend to rejoice by exchanging "high fives," in which only their hands actually touch.

It is no wonder that so many of the people in our society, particularly males, feel alienated or distanced from God, other people, and themselves. Our lack of physical spontaneity and our constricted notions of appropriate sexuality make it difficult to experience the unconditional love of God.

It is no wonder that our God sometimes seems so far away and so little a part of our daily lives.

Accept all of yourself and give all of yourself, and you will discover the love of God.

Too many people treat life as if it were an asymptote. They keep getting closer and closer to others, but they never actually touch. ⊘

Life is filled with conflicting desires: the wish to stand up for oneself, and the desire to treat others well; the wish to be monogamous, and the temptation to be unfaithful. Numerous psychologists have indicated that such conflicts are a part of the human condition and therefore, are by definition irreconcilable.

However, it seems to me that many of these apparently conflicting desires need not conflict at all. For example, the more that I am content to be myself, the less relevant becomes the conflict between standing up for myself and respecting the rights of others. Similarly, the more deeply I come to love Gwen, the more I find that being monogamous becomes a "want," rather than a "should."

Apparently, the more that I am able to be real and to live in the present, the more likely I am to find answers that transcend life's difficult questions.

Last night I dreamt of an ex-friend, a person toward whom I still harbored many ill feelings. In my dream I was not angry. I was able to understand her side of things; I was glad to see that her new life was going well and was able to let go of my anger.

In my dream, it brought me great peace simply to accept her as she was. Later, when I awoke, it brought me great peace simply to accept her as she was.

To accept oneself brings contentment. To accept others brings peace. To accept both brings a powerful gentleness and an ever-present awareness of life's beauty.

Forgiveness is *not* license. Rather, it is the realization that the only moment that matters is right now; it is the active desire to let go of the past and to live in the present, which is always new.

To punish oneself or others is to live in the past. Ø

have heard a number of people say things like, "I never intended to have an affair. It just happened." But it seems to me that we tend to find what we are looking for. It behooves us, therefore, to search only for those things that we truly want to find.

Where we look, there shall we go. Look not backwards, then, onto past mistakes and sins, but forward, toward the vision of what could be.

To dream it is to know it;
To know it is to make it yours;
To make it yours is to be able to share it with others;
Dream, therefore, of love and beauty, that your life may be filled with both.

Carl Rogers (one of my heroes) dropped out of seminary because he felt he could not work in a field in which he was required to accept a specified list of religious beliefs. Similarly, because I was an ordained minister, many of my "atheist" friends have teased me about my supposed multiple of religious beliefs and have boasted about their own lack of any fixed beliefs.

It seems to me, however, that it is actually the atheists, the supposed non-believers, who have the longest list of religious beliefs. For example they assume that God is male, judgmental, punitive and static. They attribute many different characteristics to God and then reject the existence of such a God. They probably are right to assert that their God does not exist. However, that does not mean that God does not exist. Rather, it simply indicates that their myriad of assumptions and beliefs about God are incorrect.

As I have come to be more in touch with my spiritual self, I have *not* adopted an extensive list of new beliefs. Rather, I have been able to jettison many of my previous beliefs, such as the belief that I must please everybody, that I must pretend to be somebody I am not, and that God is a punitive judge. In the place of these old beliefs have come, not additional beliefs, but rather an awareness—an awareness of God's presence and forgiveness, an awareness of my ability to love others, and an awareness that I am who I am and can be nothing else.

There are no unbelievers. There are only those with too many beliefs.

Sometimes, in just the right light, at just the right angle, my newborn daughter looks just like me. I look at her and I see myself looking back, and it always startles me. The miracle of reproduction can be a bit unnerving.

I love our new daughter. However, she requires so much of my time that it is easy for me to let slide all of the things that I really like to do. Then, when I do get a little free time, I do not know what to do with it, because I have lost touch with the things that bring me pleasure. After a while, I end up feeling as if I do not know who I am anymore.

Now I understand why so many displaced homemakers say that it takes them a long time to figure out who they are. When I consistently allow someone else's needs to come first, the *me* gets so badly lost that finding it again takes some time.

Bob Dylan, in the notes on the jacket of one of his albums, said that if he did not finish a song while he was experiencing that inspired moment, it often became a real struggle to finish the song at all. That's true for me, too. When I feel the need to write, it is not enough to jot down my main idea and to develop that idea more completely at a later time. When I do that, writing becomes a real struggle.

No amount of work can compensate for a lack of inspiration.

One would expect that after a while I would have nothing left to write. In truth, however, the more that I write the more that I have to say.

The more I write, the more I feel the need to write.

The more I feel the need to write, the better I write.

The better I write, the more willing I am to take the time when I feel the urge to write.

It is clear that my body is getting older; my knees hurt, my ankles are swollen, my eyes are bad, and I can not "play" for as long as I used to. Conversely, my spirit is getting younger; I now am much more able to be spontaneous, loving, and genuine. This all seems a bit backward, somehow, and yet I sense a certain symmetry there as well.

It seems as though my body is becoming less and less important, while my spirit is becoming more and more primary. If this process continues, the afterlife, a life centered totally in the spirit, may well seem like a natural transition, rather than a radical change. I find this thought quite comforting, somehow.

Often when I hear a couple quarreling over things such as religious differences—especially when there are children involved—it seems to me that they are trying too hard to "win" and not hard enough to love.

There are no dead ends when each person in a couple is willing to discuss a matter openly and desires above all else to treat both people lovingly.

Last month I sprained my thumb and wrist, thereby rendering my right hand nearly useless for several weeks. During those weeks, I constantly had to alter my usual way of doing things, in order to adapt to the new situation. One day, while I was trying to shovel snow with one hand, I understood why so many handicapped people get mad when able-bodied people call them "brave" or "courageous." As the handicapped people often point out, all they are trying to do is to cope as best they can with their particular situation. That is how I felt, too. Although I may have looked brave, I was no hero. I was simply a person who was trying to cope; what other option was there, really?

Several years ago, I had a job in a place where I was not truly appreciated. So, I quit. For quite a while afterwards, I sat around feeling bitter about the way that I had been treated and feeling bad about myself. Eventually, however, it occurred to me that instead of dwelling on the unfairness of this one past situation, I should look to the future; I should look for a job that would reward, rather than punish, a person with my talents. It was amazing; soon after I adopted this new attitude, I felt much more grateful for all of the blessings that I had received on other occasions, my previous employer faded into ancient history, and a number of better job possibilities did indeed appear.

Frankl often said that a person with a "why" can live with almost any "how."[5] I agree and would add that a person with an eye toward the future can overcome almost any past.

Life keeps rolling along, and I can choose either to throw myself under its wheels or to hop on and enjoy the ride.

When I accepted the job that I just mentioned, I knew that the person who was to be my supervisor had some problems. However, everything else about the job was so appealing that I chose to overlook that one negative aspect. Of course, I later came to regret my decision; I came to wonder how I could have been dumb enough to have taken that job in the first place.

I have observed a similar dynamic on other occasions. As a coin collector, if I have been looking for a certain type of coin for a long time, I am tempted to buy the first one that I come across, even if it is seriously flawed. Yet, whenever I buy such an inferior specimen, I always come to regret my decision. Every time I look at that coin, I ask myself, "Why didn't you keep looking until you found the coin you really wanted?"

Similarly, when I got married the first time, I married a woman who was a less-than-ideal mate for me. Later, of course, I came to regret that decision. Now that I am married to the woman who truly is my soul mate, I ask myself, "Why didn't you wait until you found the woman that you really wanted?"

The point, I guess, is that life has frequently taught me the same lesson, in a variety of forms. When I settle for less than what I really want, that's exactly what I get.

Life often teaches me the same lesson many times over. In other words, one of the lessons that life often teaches me is that life often teaches me the same lesson.

I love the whole idea of Christmas. I love the anticipation, the holiday spirit, and the inspirational songs. I sometimes find, however, that the closer it gets to Christmas Day, the more restless I become. I start to worry that I will not have enough time to buy all of the necessary gifts, I draw up detailed plans for our holiday trips, and I endlessly calculate whether we will have enough money to make it through the holidays.

At such times, it seems that I like the idea of Christmas a lot better than I like the reality.

This restless feeling has become a sign to me, an indication that I am living in the future, rather than in the present. It tells me that my worrying about upcoming events is interfering with my ability to simply enjoy the spirit-filled present.

Love, joy, and peace can be expressed and experienced only in the present, which explains why I get restless and unhappy when I live too much in the future.

My days are generally filled with things that I "have to do." Occasionally, however, there comes a day free of obligations—a day that I can spend in whatever way that I choose. I take great pleasure in such days. The freedom to do whatever strikes me at any given moment is very liberating for me, perhaps because it allows me to live so totally in the present. For me, at least, this simple concept—living in the present—has a power to heal that is beyond my understanding.

Just as physical exercise often leaves me feeling invigorated, rather than tired, doing "nothing in particular" often leaves me feeling energized, rather than bored.

Fear is a painfully ironic phenomenon. People who fear that they will be friendless tend either to protect themselves against rejection or to be overly friendly, both of which are likely to leave them friendless. I am afraid of dogs, and my fear of being attacked makes it more likely that a dog will indeed attack me. A person who fears not getting the anticipated job is likely to communicate that fear in an interview, and thus to increase the odds of failure. Our nation fears a military attack, and our mad scramble to build more weapons makes other nations jittery, thus increasing the likelihood that we will be attacked.

Roosevelt knew what he was talking about when he said that we have nothing to fear but fear itself. Ironically, all too often our fear dooms us to experience precisely that which we fear.

Whenever I lead a support group or a growth group, I am struck by the number of normal people who have difficulty acknowledging and expressing their own thoughts and emotions. So many people have so much trouble with the simplest thing in the world—being themselves.

The cost of pretending to be someone else, of conforming to the expectations of others, is exactly this: after pretending long enough, even we forget who we really are.

The older I get, the simpler life seems to me. I am not denying that shades of grey exist, nor am I saying that what is "right" is always obvious. I merely am saying that, at its most elemental level, life really is quite simple. It is only when we lie, pretend to be someone else, or perceive a need to protect the feelings of others that life becomes needlessly complex.

I am what I am, and the more I am content to be myself, the more I perceive life's fundamental simplicity.

We are still essentially the same creatures that we were five-hundred years ago. Our environment has become infinitely more sophisticated and complex, but we have not.

Humanity's most fundamental questions have remained much the same over the centuries, and so have most of our answers.

Fashions change, but our need to appear fashionable does not.

The way that we look does indeed convey a lot of information—not about who we are, necessarily, but about who we think we are.

When I look at a photograph of several people, one of whom is me, I hardly see the other people in the picture because I am so busy looking at myself. I make comments that sound if I am looking closely at all of the people in the picture, but only so that others will not realize how egocentric I am.

Sometimes I understand my own motivation and behavior so well that it is embarrassing.

Because I am so egocentric, my perceptions of reality are fragmentary and limited. Furthermore, these fragments of perception create within me a number of reactions and emotions, only some of which I am consciously aware. Then, when I later try to recall how I responded, I can recall only some of the reactions I had been aware of; often, I recall only one thought, image, or reaction. Finally, when I am talking to other people and trying to translate that one image into words, much of my reality gets lost in the translation.

Clearly, the road from "what actually happened" to "what I have to say about that event" is rocky indeed.

Given all of this fragmentation, my attempts to "prove" that I am "right" seem ridiculous.

I have only a fragmentary understanding of reality, and nothing could be more fragmentary than my awareness of this fact.

We are what we see. Conversely, we also see what we are.

Having a child has been incredibly rewarding for me but has also been a huge pain in the neck. This combination confuses me at times, but I get much more confused when I try to pretend that only one half of this apparent contradiction is true.

Paul Tillich said that life is ambiguous.[6] I agree with Tillich; it seems to me that I often have mixed motives and emotions and that I am most healthy when I acknowledge this fact.

Life's rewards are attained not *by* struggling but *in* struggling. It is the process itself that both defines us and rewards us.

Life *is* the reward.

To struggle endlessly just to attain a reward is to miss the real reward.

To say that the end justifies the means is to lose sight of an important point: in a fundamental way, the means *is* the end. Ø

The Old Testament includes a number of stories known as "call narratives." In these stories, God asks a heretofore unknown, little-regarded person to perform an important task. Invariably, the person's initial response is "Who, me?" They simply do not see their own tremendous potential and thus are rendered helpless. Later in the story, however, once they begin to realize that God truly believes in them, they begin to believe in themselves and they invariably— almost automatically, it seems—go on to perform great feats.

One of the greatest gifts that we can give to a person is to believe in them, to see clearly their potential greatness. For if we can help a person to see their own tremendous potential, their success is virtually assured.

To believe in someone's potential is to help make actual that potential.

Thank-you, Gwen, for seeing my potential.

Everyone has a flawed past and a radically open future, which means that it's always too late and never too late.

When Jack asked, "Why does God allow there to be pain in the world?," someone replied, "Because if we were always happy, we would not enjoy it" (a response which ignores the popularity of the climate in Southern California).

To me, this cliché response misses the point entirely. To be human is to have free will, which means that I am free to make choices. Very often, the choices that I make, such as choosing to be selfish, to interpret situations negatively, to hoard love, and to settle for short-term rewards, do indeed cause me pain, but that is my fault, not God's.

Most pain is self-inflicted.

My tendency towards perfectionism often leaves me feeling that I am not really good enough or that I do not quite measure up. This mind set prevents me from being a gracious receiver—of compliments for example—and thus eliminates the possibility of true intimacy. ✦

I no longer worry as much as I once did about whether my friends, clients, and acquaintances like me. Consequently, people now seem more inclined to like me. When I do not need something, I am much more likely to receive it.

As a counselor, all that I have to give is myself. When I give the gift of myself, I become a part of the healing process. When I withhold that self, the counseling session becomes an abstract discussion, rather than an opportunity for reconciliation.

The difference between an acquaintance and a friend is precisely this: our acquaintances can talk to us, entertain us, and even teach us, but it is our friends who can heal us.

When I lie to myself about who I am, I become distanced not only from myself but also from God, who loves me just the way I am.

For me, summer is a magical time; the cool summer mornings, with their hints of the heat to come, transport me back to the summers of my childhood, to a time when life seemed full of possibilities. I will know that I have become fully self-actualized when life's simple joys and endless possibilities are as clear to me as they were during those childhood summer mornings.

Whenever I am having difficulty choosing between two options and one of the options is unexpectedly forced upon me, I suddenly became convinced that it was the other option that I really wanted all along.

I used to regret the fact that I changed careers several times before I finally found my niche; I often lamented the time that I had "wasted" along the way. Lately, however, I have begun to see the myriad of ways in which my past experiences have contributed to my current happiness. So, I have changed my tune; now I say, "nothing is ever wasted."

Life is not a vacuum; there are no events that are uninfluenced by other events.

I frequently make the mistake of assuming too much responsibility for others. That is, I often say things like, "Oh, I couldn't say that to him/her because I wouldn't want him/her to feel bad." Although it indeed is good to care about others, it is not my job to make sure that people feel the way that they are "supposed to." There is a difference between love and control.

In truth, I cannot control the emotions, thoughts or reactions of anyone else. Thus, if I assume that it is my duty to do so, I am doomed to disappointment, frustration, and unhappiness.

If I truly love someone, I must take the risk of letting them see the real me, and I also must take the risk of letting them react, think, and feel as they do. Only by letting go of my need to control can I know love.

Oftentimes, if I cannot quit feeling a certain way, it is because I am fighting it and not allowing myself to feel that way. For example, when I was a professor, if there was a day in which a class did not go very well, I usually would try to dispense with my bad feelings too quickly. That is, I would say things to myself like, "It really did not go all that badly," "I should just concentrate on how to do things differently next time," or "It really wasn't my fault." Ironically, when I tried to get rid of my sadness and unhappiness in that way, I usually felt a bit sad and depressed all day.

Conversely, on those occasions when I admitted to myself that I felt bad and embarrassed and allowed myself to truly feel those feelings instead of defending myself against them, my depression quickly lifted, and I soon was ready to move on.

Apparently, when I try to avoid feeling pain, I merely prolong my pain.

Now, when a client asks me, "How can I stop feeling so angry?" I say, "First, you have to start."

Notes:

1. Erich Fromm, *The Art of Loving*, (New York: Bantam Books, 1963), pps. 18-21.

2. Beverly Cleary, *Ramona the Brave*, (New York: William Morrow, 1975), p. 61.

3. Hugh Prather, *Notes on Love and Courage*, (Garden City, N.Y.: Doubleday, 1977),

4. James B. Nelson, *Embodiment: An Approach to Sexuality and Christian Theology* (Minneapolis: Augsburg Publishing House, 1978) p. 26

5. Victor E. Frankl, *Man's Search for Meaning*, (New York: Washington Square Press, 1963).

6. Paul Tillich, *Systematic Theology*, Vol. III, (Chicago: University of Chicago Press, 1967).